بِسْمِ اللّٰهِ

الرَّحْمٰنِ

الرَّحِيْمِ

bismillah

ar-Rahman

ar-Raheem

(1:1) In the name of Allah,

the Most Merciful,

the Ever Merciful

Excerpt taken from <u>Tafsir Ibn Kathir (section 1.1)</u>:

"Imam Ahmad recorded in his <u>Musnad,</u> that a person who was riding behind the Prophet [PBUH] said,
'The Prophet's animal tripped, so I said, "Cursed Shaytan."

The Prophet said,

لَا تَقُلْ: تَعِسَ الشَّيْطَانُ، فَإِنَّكَ إِذَا قُلْتَ: تَعِسَ الشَّيْطَانُ، تَعَاظَمَ وَقَالَ:
«بِقُوَّتِي
صَرَعْتُهُ، وَإِذَا قُلْتَ: بِاسْمِ اللهِ تَصَاغَرَ حَتَى يَصِيرَ مِثْلَ الذُّبَابِ»

(*Do not say, 'Cursed Shaytan,' for if you say these words, Satan becomes arrogant and says, 'With my strength I made him fall.' When you say, 'Bismillah,' Satan will become as small as a fly.*)

Further, An-Nasa'i recorded in his book <u>Al-Yawm wal-Laylah</u>, and also Ibn Marduwyah in his <u>Tafsir</u> that Usamah bin `Umayr said, "I was riding behind the Prophet..." and he mentioned the rest of the above Hadith. The Prophet said in this narration,

لَا تَقُلْ هكَذَا فَإِنَّهُ يَتَعَاظَمُ حَتَّى يَكُونَ كَالْبَيْتِ، وَلكِنْ قُلْ: بِسْمِ اللهِ، فَإِنَّهُ يَصْغَرُ
حَتَّى يَكُونَ كَالذُّبَابَة

(*Do not say these words, because then Satan becomes larger; as large as a house. Rather, say, 'Bismillah,' because Satan then becomes as small as a fly.*)

This is the blessing of reciting Bismillah...
Basmalah (reciting Bismillah) is recommended before starting any action or deed."

as-selamu alaikum! May peace be upon you!

This book was created for YOU to get a little bit closer to Allah subhanahu wa ta'ala (S.W.T.) [Glorious and Exalted is He]!

Congrats on starting your next step!

There's always much more to learn and know, in shaa Allah (God-willing)!

May Allah (subhanahu wa ta'ala (S.W.T.) [Glorious and Exalted is He])

guide us towards fruitful & meaningful knowledge! Ameen!

Primary Source: for surah names in Arabic and English, # of ayat, revelation location, aya translation, and notes:

Al-Quran (2014): al-quran.info

**Each aya presented on a flashcard is the one that the surah is named after.*

Notes on Salawat:

(SAWS) or (PBUH): *Salallahu Alayhi Wa Salam* or

Peace and Blessings be Upon Him

*Said after Prophet Muhammad (PBUH) is mentioned

(AS) : ***Alayhi as-Salam*** or *may peace be upon him/her/them*

*Said after the mention of any prophet

(RA): ***radhi Allahu anhu/anha*** *or may Allah be pleased with him/her*

*Said after the mention of any respected person

Notes on the graphics:

*You can also have images on each flashcard with the

Quran Flashcards Workbook: Learn the Names of All 114 Surahs Through Image Recognition

version.

Aya & Du'a Flashcard Ideas:

→ **One at a time**

- Work on one flashcard a week, a day, a month
- Learn the same facts for all 6 surahs on a page

→ **Altogether**

- Cut out all of the same colored cards & shuffle them together

→ **Teamwork**

- Gather a group & make learning goals together

→ **Quiz Warmup**

- Start your day, lesson, learning with a flashcard review

→ **Jeopardy!**

- Lay all the cards out, shout out a fact, & earn a point for grabbing the right card

→ **Memory**

- Randomly place a number of cards out & figure out what you know the same about pairs of cards

→ **Schedule it in**

- Pick a day or time each week to enjoy cutting out the next page

→ **Bookmark**

- Use a flashcard to mark your spot in your textbooks and books

PS: IF YOU FIND ANY ERROR THAT NEEDS CORRECTING, PLEASE GET IN TOUCH: READANDRECITE.ORG

MY PROGRESS CHART for the FIRST 31.5%! 😊😊😊

1		2		3		4		5		6	
Number:		Number:		Number:		Number:		Number:		Number:	
English:		English:		English:		English:		English:		English:	
Arabic:		Arabic:		Arabic:		Arabic:		Arabic:		Arabic:	
Aya:		Aya:		Aya:		Aya:		Aya:		Aya:	

7		8		9		10		11		12	
Number:		Number:		Number:		Number:		Number:		Number:	
English:		English:		English:		English:		English:		English:	
Arabic:		Arabic:		Arabic:		Arabic:		Arabic:		Arabic:	
Aya:		Aya:		Aya:		Aya:		Aya:		Aya:	

13		14		15		16		17		18	
Number:		Number:		Number:		Number:		Number:		Number:	
English:		English:		English:		English:		English:		English:	
Arabic:		Arabic:		Arabic:		Arabic:		Arabic:		Arabic:	
Aya:		Aya:		Aya:		Aya:		Aya:		Aya:	

19		20		21		22		23		24	
Number:		Number:		Number:		Number:		Number:		Number:	
English:		English:		English:		English:		English:		English:	
Arabic:		Arabic:		Arabic:		Arabic:		Arabic:		Arabic:	
Aya:		Aya:		Aya:		Aya:		Aya:		Aya:	

25		26		27		28		29		30	
Number:		Number:		Number:		Number:		Number:		Number:	
English:		English:		English:		English:		English:		English:	
Arabic:		Arabic:		Arabic:		Arabic:		Arabic:		Arabic:	
Aya:		Aya:		Aya:		Aya:		Aya:		Aya:	

31		32		33		34		35		36	
Number:		Number:		Number:		Number:		Number:		Number:	
English:		English:		English:		English:		English:		English:	
Arabic:		Arabic:		Arabic:		Arabic:		Arabic:		Arabic:	
Aya:		Aya:		Aya:		Aya:		Aya:		Aya:	

JUZ 1: al-Fatiha 1:1 → al-Baqara 2:141

JUZ 2: al-Baqara 2:142 → al-Baqara 2:242

JUZ 3: al-Baqara 2:253 → al-Imran 3:92

JUZ 4: al-Imran 3:93 → an-Nisa 4:23

JUZ 5: an-Nisa 4:24 → an-Nisa 4:147

JUZ 6: an-Nisa 4:148 → an-Ma'ida 5:81

JUZ 7: an-Nisa 5:82 → al-An'aam 6:110

Longest Surah in Qur'an → Surah Baqara (286 ayat)

Longest Aya in Qur'an → Surah Baqara, Aya 282

When can you add more Islamic learning time to your day-to-day, in shaa Allah (God-willing)?

Promise Allah to schedule in time to study His religion this week. What day and time this week?

Next week?

Every week?

1

الْفَاتِحَة

2

الْبَقَرَة

3

آلِ عِمْرَان

4

النِّسَاء

5

الْمَائِدَة

6

الْأَنْعَام

al-Baqara 2

The Calf

AKA: The Heifer; The Cow

MEDINAN # of Ayas: 286

Longest surah!

(67) "And when Musa said to his people, 'Indeed Allah commands you to slaughter a cow,' they said, 'Do you take us in derision?' He said, 'I seek Allah's protection lest I should be one of the senseless!'"

al-Fatiha 1

The Opening

AKA: The [Lord's] Praise; The Prologue

MECCAN # of Ayas: 7

(1) "Bismillah, ar-Rahman ar-Raheem" ["in the name of Allah, the Most Merciful, the Most Compassionate"]

We should begin all things with these words, too!

an-Nisa 4

Women

AKA: The Woman

MEDINAN # of Ayas: 176

(40) "Indeed Allah does not wrong [anyone] [even to the extent of] an atom's weight, and if it be a good deed He doubles it[s reward], and gives from Himself a great reward."

**no specific aya for the name but it makes frequent reference to matters concerning women*

al-Imran 3

The Family of Imran

AKA: The House of Imran; The Imrans

MEDINAN # of Ayas: 200

(33) "Indeed Allah chose Adam and Nuh, and the progeny of Ibraheem and the progeny of Imran above all the nations;"

(34) "some of them are descendants of the others, and Allah is All-Hearing, All-Knowing."

al-An'aam 6

The Cattle

AKA: The Livestock

MECCAN # of Ayas: 165

(136) "They dedicate to Allah out of what He has created of the crops and cattle a portion, and say, 'This is for Allah,' so do they maintain, 'and this is for our partners.' But what is for their partners does not reach Allah, and what is for Allah reaches their partners. Evil is the judgement that they make."

al-Ma'ida 5

The Table

AKA: The Feast; The Table-Spread

MEDINAN # of Ayas: 120

(112) "When the Disciples said, 'O Isa son of Maryam! Can your Lord send down to us a table from the sky?' Said he, 'Be wary of Allah, should you be faithful.'"

Hadith on Reciting Ayat al-Kursi after each prayer:

Abu Umamah reported: The Messenger of Allah, peace and blessings be upon him, said, "Whoever recites the verse of the Throne (Ayat al-Kursi) after every prescribed prayer, there will be nothing standing between him and his entering Paradise except death."

Source: al-Mu'jam al-Kabīr 7406 **Grade:** Sahih (authentic) according to Al-Albani

Surah 2 (al-Baqara), aya 255:
Ayat al-Kursi / The Throne Verse

قُل هُوَ اللَّهُ أَحَدٌ

Allahu la ilaha illa huwa al-Hayya al-Qayyam

255 Allah! There is no god except Him. He is the Living One, The All-Sustainer

لا تَأْخُذُهُ سِنَةٌ وَلا نَومٌ

la takhuduhu sinatun wa la nawm

Neither drowsiness befalls Him nor sleep.

لَهُ ما فِي السَّماواتِ وَما فِي الأَرضِ

lahu ma fi samawati wa ma fil-ard

To Him belongs whatever is in the heavens and whatsoever is in the earth.

مَن ذَا الَّذي يَشفَعُ عِندَهُ إِلّا بِإِذنِهِ

man dha ladi yashfu'a 'indahu illa bi-idhnihi

Who is it that may intercede with Him except with His permission?

يَعلَمُ ما بَينَ أَيديهِم وَما خَلفَهُم

ya'lamu ma bayna 'aydihim wa ma khalfahum

He knows that which is in front of them and that which is behind them.

وَلا يُحيطونَ بِشَيءٍ مِن عِلمِهِ إِلّا بِما شاءَ

wa la yuhituna bishay'een min 'ilmihi illa bi ma shaa

And they do not comprehend anything of His knowledge except what He wishes.

وَسِعَ كُرسِيُّهُ السَّماواتِ وَالأَرضَ

wasiya kursiyyahu as-samawati wal-ard

His seat (throne) embraces the heavens and the earth

وَلا يَئودُهُ حِفظُهُما

wa la ya'uduhu hifzuhuma

and He is not wearied by their preservation

وَهُوَ العَلِيُّ العَظيمُ

wa huwa al-'Ala al-'Atheem

And He is the All-Exalted, the All-Supreme

Hadith on Reciting Ayat al-Kursi before going to sleep:

Narrated Abu Huraira: Allah's Apostle ordered me to guard the Zakat revenue of Ramadan. Then somebody came to me and started stealing of the foodstuff. I caught him and said, "I will take you to Allah's Apostle!" Then Abu Huraira described the whole narration and said:) That person said (to me), "(Please don't take me to Allah's Apostle and I will tell you a few words by which Allah will benefit you.) When you go to your bed, recite Ayat-al-Kursi (2.255) for then there will be a guard from Allah who will protect you all night long and Satan will not be able to come near you till dawn." (When the Prophet heard the story) he said (to me), "He (who came to you at night) told you the truth although he is a liar; and it was Satan."

Source: al-Bukhari,
Vol 6, Hadith #530

Grade: Sahih (authentic)

JUZ 8: al-An'aam 6:111 → al-A'raf 7:87

JUZ 9: al-A'raf 7:88 → al-Anfal 8:40

JUZ 10: al-Anfal 8:41 → at-Tawbah 9:92

JUZ 11: at-Tawbah 9:93 → Hud 11:5

JUZ 12: Hud 11:6 → Yusuf 12:52

7

الْأَعْرَاف

8

الْأَنْفَال

9

التَّوْبَة

10

يُونُس

11

هُود

12

يُوسُف

al-Anfal 8

The Spoils

AKA: Battle Gains; The Spoils of War

MEDINAN # of Ayas: 75

(1) "They ask you concerning the anfal. Say, 'The anfal belong to Allah and the Apostle.' So be wary of Allah and settle your differences, and obey Allah and His Apostle, should you be faithful."

al-A'Raf 7

The Elevations

AKA: The Heights

MECCAN # of Ayas: 206

(8) "The weighing [of deeds] on that Day is a truth. As for those whose deeds weigh heavy in the scales — it is they who are the felicitous."

...

(46) "And there will be a veil between them. And on the Elevations will be certain men who recognize each of them by their mark. They will call out to the inhabitants of paradise, 'Peace be to you!' (They will not have entered it, though they would be eager to do so."

Yunus 10

Jonah

MECCAN # of Ayas: 109

(98) "Why has there not been any town that might believe, so that its belief might benefit it, except the people of Yunus? When they believed, We removed from them the punishment of disgrace in the life of this world, and We provided for them for a while."

at-Tawbah 9

Repentance

AKA: Dispensation; Immunity

MEDINAN # of Ayas: 129

(3) "[This is] an announcement from Allah and His Apostle to all the people on the day of the greater Hajj that Allah and His Apostle repudiate the polytheists: If you repent that is better for you; but if you turn your backs [on Allah], know that you cannot thwart Allah, and inform the faithless of a painful punishment"

Yusuf 12

Joseph

MECCAN # of Ayas: 111

(7) "In Yusuf and his brothers there are certainly signs for the seekers."

**no specific aya for the name but the story of Yusuf (AS) is highlighted here*

Hud 11

Hud

AKA: The Prophet Hud

MECCAN # of Ayas: 123

(50) "And to 'Ad [We sent] Hud, their brother. He said, 'O my people! Worship Allah. You have no other god besides Him: you merely fabricate [the deities that you worship]."

BRIEF NOTES:

Surah 8: an-Anfal (The Spoils)

Material gains (people & possessions) after the Battle of Badr (mentioned directly 3:123-125) are distributed fairly to those who fought for the cause of Allah (SWT) because of these ayas.

Surah 10: Yunus (AS)

Prophet Jonah (AS) is known as ذُو ٱلنُّونْ (Dhul-Nūn): "The One of the Fish [or whale]" in 21:87 and 68:48. He was tossed overboard and calls out to his Lord in repentance. His mention also appears in: 4:163; 6:86; 10:98; 37:139-148; 68:48-50.

Surah 11: Hud (AS)

Prophet Hud (AS) guides his people to worship only Allah (SWT) but the people refuse so they are punished with a severe drought and a "furious violent wind" [as mentioned in al-Haqqah (69:6-8)]: More on Hud (AS) found in: 11:50-57; 23:33-38; 46:24-25; 69:6-7.

Surah 12: Yusuf (AS)

Prophet Ya'qub (AS) interprets his son's [Prophet Yusuf (AS)] dream that he'll become a prophet. Yusuf's brothers become jealous & throw him down a well. He is rescued but sent to Egypt. Later he interprets dreams of the king. He becomes the king himself. Prophet Yusuf (AS) and his father (AS) are eventually reunited. There's much more to his story: 12:3-104; 6:84; 40:34

Surah 12 (Yusuf) (AS): aya 101
du'a of Yusuf (AS)

رَبِّ قَدْ آتَيْتَنِي مِنَ الْمُلْكِ وَعَلَّمْتَنِي مِن تَأْوِيلِ الْأَحَادِيثِ ۚ فَاطِرَ السَّمَاوَاتِ وَالْأَرْضِ أَنتَ وَلِيِّي فِي الدُّنْيَا وَالْآخِرَةِ ۖ تَوَفَّنِي مُسْلِمًا وَأَلْحِقْنِي بِالصَّالِحِينَ

rabbi qad ʾātaytanī mina l-mulki wa-ʿallamtanī min taʾwīli l-aḥādīthi fāṭira s-samāwāti wa-l-ʾarḍi ʾanta waliyyī fī d-dunyā wa-l-ʾākhirati tawaffanī musliman wa-ʾalḥiqnī bi-ṣ-ṣāliḥīn

101 'My Lord! You have granted me a share in the kingdom, and taught me the interpretation of dreams. Originator of the heavens and earth! You are my guardian in this world and the Hereafter! Let my death be in submission [to You], and unite me with the Righteous.'

Surah 7 (al-A'Raf): aya 23
du'a of Adam (AS) and Hawwa (RA)

قالا رَبَّنا ظَلَمنا أَنفُسَنا وَإِن لَم تَغفِر لَنا وَتَرحَمنا لَنَكونَنَّ مِنَ الخاسِرينَ

qālā rabbanā ẓalamnā ʾanfusanā wa-ʾin lam taghfir lanā wa-tarḥamnā la-nakūnanna mina l-khāsirīn

23 They said, 'Our Lord, we have wronged ourselves! If You do not forgive us and have mercy upon us, we will surely be among the losers.'

Surah 11 (Hud) (AS) : aya 47
du'a of Nuh (AS)

قالَ رَبِّ إِنّي أَعوذُ بِكَ أَن أَسأَلَكَ ما لَيسَ لي بِهِ عِلمٌ وَإِلّا تَغفِر لي وَتَرحَمني أَكُن مِنَ الخاسِرين

qāla rabbi ʾinnī ʾaʿūdhu bika ʾan ʾasʾalaka mā laysa lī bihī ʿilmun wa-ʾillā taghfir lī wa-tarḥamnī ʾakun mina l-khāsirīn

47 He said, 'My Lord! I seek Your protection lest I should ask You something of which I have no knowledge. If You do not forgive me and have mercy upon me,

JUZ 13: Yusuf 12:53 → Ibraheem 14:52

JUZ 14: al-Hijr 15:1 → An-Nahl 16:128

JUZ 15: al-Isra' 17:1 → Al-Kahf 18:74

There is SO MUCH MORE information found in the Qur'an than on these modest notes about it. Read a little more of each surahs and take notes:

13

الرَّعْد

14

إبْرَاهِيم

15

الْحِجْر

16

النَّحْل

17

الْإسْرَاء

18

الْكَهْف

Ibraheem 14

Abraham

MECCAN # of Ayas: 52

(35) "When Ibraheem said, 'My Lord! Make this city a sanctuary, and save me and my children from worshiping idols.'"

al-R'ad 13

Thunder

MEDINAN # of Ayas: 43

(13) "The thunder celebrates His praise, and the angels [too], in awe of Him, and He releases the thunderbolts and strikes with them whomever He wishes. Yet they dispute concerning Allah, though He is great in might."

an-Nahl 16

The Bee

MECCAN # of Ayas: 128

(68) "And your Lord inspired the bee [saying]: 'Make your home in the mountains, and on the trees and the trellises that they erect."

(69) "Then eat from every [kind of] fruit and follow meekly the ways of your Lord.' There issues from its belly a juice of diverse hues in which there is a cure for the people. There is indeed a sign in that for a people who reflect."

al-Hijr 15

Hijr

AKA: Stoneland; The Rocky Tract; The Stone Valley

MECCAN # of Ayas: 99

(80) "Certainly the inhabitants of Hijr denied the apostles."

(81) "We had given them Our signs but they disregarded them."

al-Kahf 18

The Cave

MECCAN # of Ayas: 110

(9) " Do you suppose that the Companions of the Cave and the Inscription were among Our wonderful signs?"

(10) " When the youths took refuge in the Cave, they said, 'Our Lord! Grant us a mercy from Yourself, and help us on to rectitude in our affair.'"

al-Isra' 17

The Night Journey

AKA: Glory; The Children of Israel

MECCAN # of Ayas: 111

(1) " Immaculate is He who carried His servant on a journey by night from the Sacred Mosque to the Farthest Mosque whose environs We have blessed, that We might show him some of Our signs. Indeed He is the All-Hearing, the All-Seeing."

BRIEF NOTES:

Surah 14: Ibraheem (AS)

There are well over 100 ayas and hadith that prove the unwavering faith of Prophet Ibraheem (AS). Some reminders of his faith are of sacrifice (like 'Eid al-Adha 37:100-111) & the building of Ka'bah (2:125-132).

Surah 13 (ar-R'ad): ayat 27-28

وَيَقُولُ الَّذِينَ كَفَرُوا لَوْلَا أُنزِلَ عَلَيْهِ آيَةٌ مِّن رَّبِّهِ ۗ قُلْ إِنَّ اللَّهَ يُضِلُّ مَن
يَشَاءُ وَيَهْدِي إِلَيْهِ مَنْ أَنَابَ

wa-yaqūlu lladhīna kafarū law-lā ʾunzila ʿalayhi ʾāyatun min rabbihī qul ʾinna llāha yuḍillu man yashāʾu wa-yahdī ʾilayhi man ʾanāb

27 The faithless say, 'Why has not some sign been sent down to him from his Lord?' Say, 'Indeed Allah leads astray whomever He wishes, and guides to Himself those who turn penitently [to Him]

الَّذِينَ آمَنُوا وَتَطْمَئِنُّ قُلُوبُهُم بِذِكْرِ اللَّهِ ۗ أَلَا بِذِكْرِ اللَّهِ تَطْمَئِنُّ الْقُلُوبُ

lladhīna ʾāmanū wa-taṭmaʾinnu qulūbuhum bi-dhikri llāhi ʾa-lā bi-dhikri llāhi taṭmaʾinnu l-qulūb

28 —those who have faith, and whose hearts find rest in the remembrance of Allah.' 'Look! The hearts find rest in Allah's remembrance!

Surah 14 (Ibraheem): aya 38
du'a of Ibraheem (AS)

رَبَّنَا إِنَّكَ تَعلَمُ ما نُخفي وَما نُعلِنُ ۗ
وَما يَخفىٰ عَلَى اللَّهِ مِن شَيءٍ فِي الأَرضِ وَلا فِي السَّماءِ

rabbanā ʾinnaka taʿlamu mā nukhfī wa-mā nuʿlinu wa-mā yakhfā ʿalā llāhi min shayʾin fī l-ʾarḍi wa-lā fī s-samāʾ

38 Our Lord! Indeed You know whatever we hide and whatever we disclose, and nothing is hidden from Allah on the earth or in the sky.

Surah 17 (al-Isra'): aya 80
du'a of Muhammad (SAWS)

وَقُل رَبِّ أَدخِلني مُدخَلَ صِدقٍ وَأَخرِجني مُخرَجَ صِدقٍ
وَاجعَل لي مِن لَدُنكَ سُلطانًا نَصيرًا

wa-qul rabbi ʾadkhilnī mudkhala ṣidqin wa-ʾakhrijnī mukhraja ṣidqin wa-jʿal lī min ladunka sulṭānan naṣīra

80 And say, 'My Lord! 'Admit me with a worthy entrance, and bring me out with a worthy departure, and render me a favorable authority from Yourself.'

JUZ 16: al-Kahf 18:75 → Ta Ha 20:135

JUZ 17: al-Anbiya 21:1 → Al-Hajj 22:78

JUZ 18: al-Mu'minun 23:1 → Al-Furqan 25:20

What word, aya, and/or surah will you learn next

for the sake of Allah SWT next?

Letter (sounds/shapes): ______________________________

Word: ______________________________

Aya: ______________________________

Surah: ______________________________

19

مَرْيَم

20

طه

21

الْأَنْبِيَاء

22

الْحَجّ

23

الْمُؤْمِنُون

24

النُّور

Ta Ha

20

Ta Ha

AKA: Ta-Ha; Taa Haa

MECCAN # of Ayas: 135

(1) "Ta Ha!"
(2) "We did not send down to you the Qur'an that you should be miserable,"
(3) "but only as an admonition to him who fears [his Lord]."

Maryam

19

Maryam

MECCAN # of Ayas: 98

(16) "And mention in the Book Maryam, when she withdrew from her family to an easterly place."

al-Hajj

22

The Pilgrimage

MEDINAN # of Ayas: 78

(26) "When We settled for Ibraheem the site of the House [saying], Do not ascribe any partners to Me, and purify My House for those who go around it, and those who stand [in it for prayer], and those who bow and prostrate."

al-Anbiya

21

The Prophets

MECCAN # of Ayas: 112

(48) "Certainly We gave Musa and Harun the Criterion, a light and reminder for the Godwary."

an-Nur

24

The Light

MEDINAN # of Ayas: 64

The Light Verse 24:35-

"Allah is the Light of the heavens and the earth. The parable of His Light is a niche wherein is a lamp — the lamp is in a glass, the glass as it were a glittering star— lit from a blessed olive tree, neither eastern nor western, whose oil almost lights up, though fire should not touch it. Light upon light. Allah guides to His Light whomever He wishes. Allah draws parables for mankind and Allah has knowledge of all things."

al-Mu'minun

23

The Faithful

AKA: The Believers; The True Believers

MECCAN # of Ayas: 118

(1) "Certainly, the faithful have attained salvation"

BRIEF NOTES:

Surah 19: Maryam (AS)

Maryam (AS) is blessed with the miraculous birth of Prophet Isa (Jesus) (AS). Maryam (AS) is the only women mentioned by name in the Qur'an. Her name appears 34 times and other ayas identifying her are mentioned often: 66:11-12, 3:37

Surah 21: an-Anbiya (The Prophets)

Presented here are 16 Prophets & Maryam (may peace be upon them all).

Surah 19 (Maryam) (AS): aya 4
du'a of Zakariya (AS)

قَالَ رَبِّ إِنِّي وَهَنَ الْعَظْمُ مِنِّي وَاشْتَعَلَ الرَّأْسُ شَيْبًا
وَلَمْ أَكُن بِدُعَائِكَ رَبِّ شَقِيًّا

qāla rabbi ʾinnī wahana l-ʿaẓmu minnī wa-shtaʿala r-raʾsu shayban wa-lam ʾakun bi-duʿāʾika rabbi shaqiyya

4 He said, 'My Lord! Indeed my bones have become feeble, and my head has turned white with age, yet never have I, my Lord, been disappointed in supplicating You!

Surah 23 (al-Mu'minun): ayat 93, 94, 97
du'a of Muhammad (SAWS)

قُل رَبِّ إِمّا تُرِيَنّي ما يوعَدونَ

qul rabbi ʾimmā turiyannī mā yūʿadūn

93 Say, 'My Lord! If You should show me what they are promised,

وَقُل رَبِّ أَعوذُ بِكَ مِن هَمَزاتِ الشَّياطينِ

rabbi fa-lā tajʿalnī fī l-qawmi ẓ-ẓālimīn

94 then do not put me, my Lord, among the wrongdoing lot.'

...

وَقُل رَبِّ أَعوذُ بِكَ مِن هَمَزاتِ الشَّياطينِ

wa-qul rabbi ʾaʿūdhu bika min hamazāti sh-shayāṭīn

97 And say, 'My Lord! I seek Your protection from the promptings of devils;

أَعوذُ بِكَ رَبِّ أَن يَحضُرونِ

wa-ʾaʿūdhu bika rabbi ʾan yaḥḍurūn

98 and I seek Your protection, my Lord, from their presence near me.'

Surah 23 (al-Mu'minun): aya 118

وَقُل رَبِّ اغفِر وَارحَم وَأَنتَ خَيرُ الرّاحِمينَ

wa-qul rabbi ghfir wa-rḥam wa-ʾanta khayru r-rāḥimīn

118 Say, 'My Lord, forgive and have mercy, and You are the best of the merciful.'

JUZ 19: al-Furqan 25:21 → an-Naml 27:55

JUZ 20: an-Naml 25:21 → al-Ankaboot 29:45

Quick Trivia!

How many surah are in the Qur'an? __________

How many ayas are in the Qur'an? __________

How many juz are in the Qur'an? __________

25

الْفُرْقَان

26

الشُّعَرَاء

27

النَّمْل

28

الْقَصَص

29

الْعَنْكَبُوت

30

الرُّوم

al-Furqan 25

The Criterion

AKA: The Standard; The Differentiator

MECCAN # of Ayas: 77

(1) "Blessed is He who sent down the Criterion to His servant that he may be a warner to all the nations."

ash-Shu'ara 26

The Poets

MECCAN # of Ayas: 227

(7) "Have they not regarded the earth, how many We have caused to grow in it of every splendid kind [of vegetation]?"

(8) " There is indeed a sign in that; but most of them do not have faith."

...

(224) "As for the poets, [only] the perverse follow them."

an-Naml 27

The Ants

MECCAN # of Ayas: 93

(17) "[Once] Solomon's hosts were marched out for him, comprising jinn, humans, and birds, and they were held in check."

(18) "When they came to the Valley of Ants, an ant said, 'O ants! Enter your dwellings, lest Solomon and his hosts should trample on you while they are unaware.'"

al-Qasas 28

The Story

AKA: The History; The Narrations

MECCAN # of Ayas: 88

(25) "Then one of the two women approached him, walking bashfully. She said, 'Indeed my father invites you to pay you the wages for watering [our flock] for us.' So when he came to him and recounted the story to him, he said, 'Do not be afraid. You have been delivered from the wrongdoing lot.'"

al-Ankaboot 29

The Spider

MECCAN # of Ayas: 69

(41) "The parable of those who take guardians instead of Allah is that of the spider that takes a home, and indeed the frailest of homes is the home of a spider, had they known!"

ar-Rum 30

The Romans

AKA: Rome; The Byzantines

MECCAN # of Ayas: 60

(2) "Byzantium has been vanquished"

(3) "in a nearby territory, but following their defeat they will be victors"

(4) "in a few years. All command belongs to Allah, before and after, and on that day the faithful will rejoice"

(4) "at Allah's help. He helps whomever He wishes, and He is the All-Mighty, the All-Merciful."

Surah 25 (al-Furqan): aya 63-66

وَعِبادُ الرَّحمٰنِ الَّذينَ يَمشونَ عَلَى الأَرضِ هَونًا

وَإِذا خاطَبَهُمُ الجاهِلونَ قالوا سَلامًا

wa-ʿibādu r-raḥmāni lladhīna yamshūna ʿalā l-ʾarḍi hawnan wa-ʾidhā khāṭabahumu l-jāhilūna qālū salāma

63 The servants of the All-beneficent are those who walk humbly on the earth, and when the ignorant address them, say, 'Peace!'

وَالَّذينَ يَبيتونَ لِرَبِّهِم سُجَّدًا وَقِيامًا

wa-lladhīna yabītūna li-rabbihim sujjadan wa-qiyāma

64 Those who spend the night for their Lord, prostrating and standing [in worship].

وَالَّذينَ يَقولونَ رَبَّنَا اصرِف عَنّا عَذابَ جَهَنَّمَ ۖ إِنَّ عَذابَها كانَ غَرامًا

wa-lladhīna yaqūlūna rabbanā ṣrif ʿannā ʿadhāba jahannama ʾinna ʿadhābahā kāna gharāma

65 Those who say, 'Our Lord! Turn away from us the punishment of hell. Indeed its punishment is enduring.

إِنَّها ساءَت مُستَقَرًّا وَمُقامًا

ʾinnahā sāʾat mustaqarran wa-muqāma

66 Indeed it is an evil abode and place.'

Surah 27 (an-Naml): aya 19
du'a of Suleiman (AS)

فَتَبَسَّمَ ضاحِكًا مِن قَولِها وَقالَ رَبِّ أَوزِعني أَن أَشكُرَ نِعمَتَكَ الَّتي أَنعَمتَ عَلَيَّ وَعَلىٰ والِدَيَّ وَأَن أَعمَلَ صالِحًا تَرضاهُ وَأَدخِلني بِرَحمَتِكَ في عِبادِكَ الصّالِحينَ

fa-tabassama ḍāḥikan min qawlihā wa-qāla rabbi ʾawziʿnī ʾan ʾashkura niʿmataka llatī ʾanʿamta ʿalayya wa-ʿalā wālidayya wa-ʾan ʾaʿmala ṣāliḥan tarḍāhu wa-ʾadkhilnī bi-raḥmatika fī ʿibādika ṣ-ṣāliḥīn

19 Whereat he smiled, amused at its words, and he said, 'My Lord! Inspire me to give thanks for Your blessing with which You have blessed me and my parents, and that I may do righteous deeds which may please You, and admit me, by Your mercy, among Your righteous servants.'

Surah 28 (al-Qasas): aya 16-17 + aya 24
du'a of Musa (AS)

قالَ رَبِّ إِنّي ظَلَمتُ نَفسي فَاغفِر لي فَغَفَرَ لَهُ ۚ إِنَّهُ هُوَ الغَفورُ الرَّحيمُ

qāla rabbi ʾinnī ẓalamtu nafsī faghfir lī fa-ghafara lahū ʾinnahū huwa l-ghafūru r-raḥīm

16 He said, 'My Lord! I have wronged myself. Forgive me!' So He forgave him. Indeed He is the All-forgiving, the All-Merciful.

قالَ رَبِّ بِما أَنعَمتَ عَلَيَّ فَلَن أَكونَ ظَهيرًا لِلمُجرِمينَ

qāla rabbi bi-mā ʾanʿamta ʿalayya fa-lan ʾakūna ẓahīran li-l-mujrimīn

17 He said, 'My Lord! As You have blessed me, I will never be a supporter of the guilty.'

...

فَسَقىٰ لَهُما ثُمَّ تَوَلّىٰ إِلَى الظِّلِّ

فَقالَ رَبِّ إِنّي لِما أَنزَلتَ إِلَيَّ مِن خَيرٍ فَقيرٌ

fa-saqā lahumā thumma tawallā ʾilā ẓ-ẓilli fa-qāla rabbi ʾinnī li-mā ʾanzalta ʾilayya min khayrin faqīr

24 So he watered [their flock] for them.
Then he withdrew toward the shade and said,
'My Lord! I am indeed in need of any good You may send down to me!'

JUZ 21: al-Ankaboot 29:46 → al-Ahzab 33:30

JUZ 22: al-Ahzab 33:31 → Ya Sin 36:27

31

لقْمَان

32

السَّجْدَة

33

الْأَحْزَاب

34

سَبَأ

35

فَاطِر

36

يس

as-Sajdah 32

Prostration

AKA: Bowing Down in Worship; The Adoration

MECCAN # of Ayas: 30

(15) "Only those believe in Our signs who, when they are reminded of them, fall down in prostration and celebrate the praise of their Lord, and they are not arrogant."

Luqman 31

Luqman

MECCAN # of Ayas: 34

(12) "Certainly We gave Luqman wisdom, saying, 'Give thanks to Allah; and whoever gives thanks, gives thanks only for his own sake. And whoever is ungrateful, [let him know that] Allah is indeed All-Sufficient, All-Laudable.'"

Saba 34

Sheba **AKA: The City of Sheba**

MECCAN # of Ayas: 54

(15) "There was certainly a sign for Saba in their habitation: two gardens, to the right and to the left. 'Eat of the provision of your Lord and give Him thanks: a good land and an All-Forgiving Lord!'"

(16) "But they disregarded [the path of Allah], so We unleashed upon them a violent flood and replaced their two gardens with two gardens bearing bitter fruit, tamarisk, and sparse lote trees"

al-Ahzab 33

The Confederates

AKA: The Allied Troops; The Joint Forces

MEDINAN # of Ayas: 73

(20) "They suppose the confederates have not left yet, and were the confederates to come [again], they would wish they were in the desert with the Bedouins asking about your news, and if they were with you they would fight but a little."

Ya Sin 36

Ya Sin

MECCAN # of Ayas: 83

(1) "Ya Sin!"

(2) "By the Wide Qur'an"

(3) "you are indeed one of the apostles,"

(4) "on a straight path."

Fatir 35

The Originator

AKA: The Bringer into Being; The Creator

MECCAN # of Ayas: 45

(1) "All praise belongs to Allah, originator of the heavens and the earth, maker of the angels [His] messengers, possessing wings, two, three or four [of them]. He adds to the creation whatever He wishes. Indeed Allah has power over all things."

Add at least 5 more character traits:

Honesty Humility Generosity Kindness Grace

Faith Sincerity Self-Control Bravery

________ ________ ________ ________ ________

________ ________ ________ ________

Which trait can you improve in yourself for the sake of Allah (SWT)?

____

____

____

____

____

Surah 33 (Al-Ahzab): ayat 1-3

يا أَيُّهَا النَّبِيُّ اتَّقِ اللَّهَ وَلا تُطِعِ الكافِرينَ وَالمُنافِقينَ ۗ إِنَّ اللَّهَ كانَ عَليمًا حَكيمًا

yā-ʾayyuhā n-nabiyyu ttaqi llāha wa-lā tuṭiʿi l-kāfirīna wa-l-munāfiqīna ʾinna llāha kāna ʿalīman ḥakīma

1 O Prophet! Be wary of Allah and do not obey the faithless and the hypocrites. Indeed Allah is All-Knowing, All-Wise.

وَاتَّبِع ما يوحىٰ إِلَيكَ مِن رَبِّكَ ۚ إِنَّ اللَّهَ كانَ بِما تَعمَلونَ خَبيرًا

wa-ttabiʿ mā yūḥā ʾilayka min rabbika ʾinna llāha kāna bi-mā taʿmalūna khabīra

2 And follow that which is revealed to you from your Lord. Indeed Allah is well aware of what you do.

وَتَوَكَّل عَلَى اللَّهِ ۚ وَكَفىٰ بِاللَّهِ وَكيلًا

wa-tawakkal ʿalā llāhi wa-kafā bi-llāhi wakīla

3 And put your trust in Allah; Allah suffices as trustee.

JUZ 23: Ya Sin 36:28 → az-Zumar 39:31

JUZ 24: az-Zumar 39:32 → Fussilat 41:46

37

الصَّافَّات

38

ص

39

الزُّمَر

40

غَافِر

41

فُصِّلَت

42

الشُّورَى

Saad

38

Saad

MECCAN # of Ayas: 88

(1) "Saad. By the Qur'an bearing the Reminder!"

as-Saffat

37

Devotional Ranks

AKA: Ranged in Rows; Drawn Up in Ranks

MECCAN # of Ayas: 182

(1) " By the [angels] ranged in ranks,"

(2) "by the ones who drive vigorously,"

(3) "by the ones who recite the reminder:"

(4) "indeed your God is certainly One,"

Ghafir

40

The Forgiver

AKA: The Forgiving One

MECCAN # of Ayas: 85

(2) "The [gradual] sending down of the Book is from Allah, the All-Mighty, the All-Knowing,"

(3) "Forgiver of Sins and Acceptor of Repentance, severe in retribution, [yet] All-Bountiful, there is no god except Him, [and] toward Him is the destination."

az-Zumar

39

The Throngs

AKA: The Crowds; The Multitudes

MECCAN # of Ayas: 75

(73) "Those who are wary of their Lord will be led to paradise in throngs. When they reach it, and its gates are opened, its keepers will say to them, 'Peace be to you! You are welcome! Enter it to remain [forever].'"

ash-Shura

42

Consultation

AKA: The Counsel

MECCAN # of Ayas: 53

(37) "Those who avoid major sins and indecencies, and forgive when angered;"

(38) "those who answer their Lord, maintain the prayer, and their affairs are by counsel among themselves, and they spend out of what We have provided them with;"

(39) "those who, when visited by aggression, come to each other's aid."

Fussilat

41

The Well-Explained

AKA: Clearly Spelled Out; Distinguished

MECCAN # of Ayas: 54

(3) "[this is] a Book whose signs have been elaborated, an Arabic Qurʾān, for a people who have knowledge,"

How do the ayas below make you feel about how it is in our world today?

Surah 41: al-Fussilat (The Well-Explained)

(43) "Nothing is said to you except what has already been said [earlier] to the apostles before you. Indeed your Lord is forgiving and One who metes out a painful retribution."

(44) "Had We made it a non-Arabic Qurʾan, they would have surely said, 'Why have not its signs been articulated?' 'What! A non-Arabian [scripture] and an Arabian [prophet]!?' Say, 'For those who have faith, it is a guidance and healing; but as for those who are faithless, there is a deafness in their ears and it is lost to their sight.' They are [as if they were] called from a distant place."

(45) "Certainly We gave Musa the Book, but differences arose about it; and were it not for a prior decree of your Lord, judgement would have been made between them, for they are indeed in grave doubt concerning it."

(46) "Whoever acts righteously, it is for his own soul, and whoever does evil, it is to its detriment, and your Lord is not tyrannical to the servants."

Surah 41 (Fussilat): aya 34

وَلَا تَسْتَوِي الْحَسَنَةُ وَلَا السَّيِّئَةُ ادْفَعْ بِالَّتِي هِيَ أَحْسَنُ
فَإِذَا الَّذِي بَيْنَكَ وَبَيْنَهُ عَدَاوَةٌ كَأَنَّهُ وَلِيٌّ حَمِيمٌ

wa-lā tastawī l-ḥasanatu wa-lā s-sayyiʾatu dfaʿ bi-llatī hiya ʾaḥsanu fa-ʾidhā lladhī baynaka wa-baynahū ʿadāwatun ka-ʾannahū waliyyun ḥamīm

34 Good and evil [conduct] are not equal.
Repel [evil] with what is best.
[If you do so,] behold, he between whom and you was enmity,
will be as though he were a sympathetic friend.

Surah 39 (az-Zumar): aya 10

قُل يا عِبادِ الَّذينَ آمَنُوا اتَّقوا رَبَّكُم ۚ لِلَّذينَ أَحسَنوا في هٰذِهِ الدُّنيا
حَسَنَةٌ ۗ وَأَرضُ اللَّهِ واسِعَةٌ ۗ إِنَّما يُوَفَّى الصّابِرونَ أَجرَهُم بِغَيرِ حِسابٍ

qul yā-ʿibādi lladhīna ʾāmanū ttaqū rabbakum li-lladhīna ʾaḥsanū fī hādhihi d-dunyā ḥasanatun wa-ʾarḍu llāhi wāsiʿatun ʾinnamā yuwaffā ṣ-ṣābirūna ʾajrahum bi-ghayri ḥisāb

10 Say, '[Allah declares:] "O My servants who have faith!
Be wary of your Lord. For those who do good in this world
there will be a good [reward], and Allah's earth is vast.
Indeed the patient will be paid in full their reward without any reckoning."'

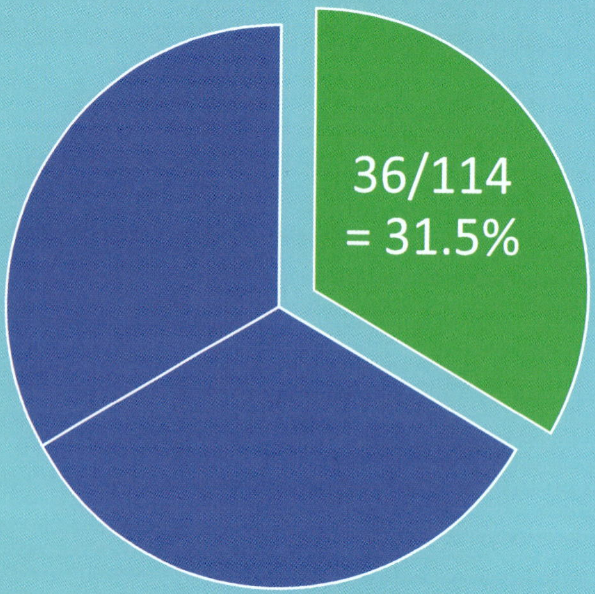

MABROOK! CONGRATULATIONS!

You've made it nearly **one third** of the way!

Alhamdullilah! (All praise is due to Allah!)

KEEP GOING! *You can do it!* in shaa Allah (God-Willing)

MY PROGRESS CHART for the SECOND 31.5%!

37		38		39		40		41		42	
Number:		Number:		Number:		Number:		Number:		Number:	
English:		English:		English:		English:		English:		English:	
Arabic:		Arabic:		Arabic:		Arabic:		Arabic:		Arabic:	
Aya:		Aya:		Aya:		Aya:		Aya:		Aya:	

43		44		45		46		47		48	
Number:		Number:		Number:		Number:		Number:		Number:	
English:		English:		English:		English:		English:		English:	
Arabic:		Arabic:		Arabic:		Arabic:		Arabic:		Arabic:	
Aya:		Aya:		Aya:		Aya:		Aya:		Aya:	

49		50		51		52		53		54	
Number:		Number:		Number:		Number:		Number:		Number:	
English:		English:		English:		English:		English:		English:	
Arabic:		Arabic:		Arabic:		Arabic:		Arabic:		Arabic:	
Aya:		Aya:		Aya:		Aya:		Aya:		Aya:	

55		56		57		58		59		60	
Number:		Number:		Number:		Number:		Number:		Number:	
English:		English:		English:		English:		English:		English:	
Arabic:		Arabic:		Arabic:		Arabic:		Arabic:		Arabic:	
Aya:		Aya:		Aya:		Aya:		Aya:		Aya:	

61		62		63		64		65		66	
Number:		Number:		Number:		Number:		Number:		Number:	
English:		English:		English:		English:		English:		English:	
Arabic:		Arabic:		Arabic:		Arabic:		Arabic:		Arabic:	
Aya:		Aya:		Aya:		Aya:		Aya:		Aya:	

67		68		69		70		71		72	
Number:		Number:		Number:		Number:		Number:		Number:	
English:		English:		English:		English:		English:		English:	
Arabic:		Arabic:		Arabic:		Arabic:		Arabic:		Arabic:	
Aya:		Aya:		Aya:		Aya:		Aya:		Aya:	

JUZ 25: Fussilat 41:47 → al-Jathiyah 45:37

JUZ 26: al-Ahqaf 46:1 → adh-Dhariyat 51:30

Make a list of good deeds you can do right now, real soon, and in the future in shaa Allah all for the sake of Allah (SWT)!

Good deeds I can do right now:

Good deeds I can do real soon:

Good deeds I want to do in the future:

43

الْزُّخْرُف

44

الْدُّخَان

45

الْجَاثِيَة

46

الْأَحْقَاف

47

مُحَمَّد

48

الْفَتْح

ad-Dukhan 44

Smoke

AKA: Mist

MECCAN # of Ayas: 59

(10) "So watch out for the day when the sky brings on a manifest smoke,"

(11) "enveloping the people. [They will cry out:] 'This is a painful punishment."

(12) "Our Lord! Remove from us this punishment. Indeed we have believed!'"

az-Zukhruf 43

The Gold Adornments

AKA: Luxury; The Gold Ornaments

MECCAN # of Ayas: 89

(35) "and ornaments of gold; yet all that would be nothing but the wares of the life of this world, and the Hereafter near your Lord is for the Godwary."

al-Ahqaf 46

The Dune Valleys of Ahqaf

AKA: The Sand Dunes; Winding Sand-Tracts

MECCAN # of Ayas: 35

(21) "And mention [Hud] the brother of 'Ad, when he warned his people at Ahqaf—and warners have passed away before and after him—saying, 'Do not worship anyone but Allah. Indeed I fear for you the punishment of a tremendous day.'"

al-Jathiyah 45

The Kneeling Down

AKA: Crouching; Bowing the Knee

MECCAN # of Ayas: 37

(28) "And you will see every nation fallen on its knees. Every nation will be summoned to its book: 'Today you will be requited for what you used to do.

(29) " 'This is Our book, which speaks truly against you. Indeed We used to record what you used to do.'"

al-Fateh 48

Victory

AKA: Conquest; The Manifest Triumph

MEDINAN # of Ayas: 29

(1) "Indeed We have inaugurated for you a clear victory,"

(2) "that Allah may forgive you what is past of your sin and what is to come, and that He may perfect His blessing upon you and guide you on a straight path,"

(3) "and Allah will help you with a mighty help."

Muhammad 47

Muhammad

MEDINAN # of Ayas: 38

(2) "But those who have faith and do righteous deeds and believe in what has been sent down to Muhammad—and it is the truth from their Lord—He shall absolve them of their misdeeds and set right their affairs."

BRIEF NOTES:

Surah 48: al-Fateh (the Victory)

The "clear victory" in aya 1 refers to Muhammad (PBUH) securing a truce guaranteeing the Muslim's rights to perform Hajj and go to the Kaaba religiously.

Surah 46 (al-Ahqaf): aya 15

وَوَصَّيْنَا الْإِنْسَانَ بِوَالِدَيْهِ إِحْسَانًا ۖ حَمَلَتْهُ أُمُّهُ كُرْهًا وَوَضَعَتْهُ كُرْهًا ۖ وَحَمْلُهُ وَفِصَالُهُ ثَلَاثُونَ شَهْرًا ۚ حَتَّىٰ إِذَا بَلَغَ أَشُدَّهُ وَبَلَغَ أَرْبَعِينَ سَنَةً قَالَ رَبِّ أَوْزِعْنِي أَنْ أَشْكُرَ نِعْمَتَكَ الَّتِي أَنْعَمْتَ عَلَيَّ وَعَلَىٰ وَالِدَيَّ وَأَنْ أَعْمَلَ صَالِحًا تَرْضَاهُ وَأَصْلِحْ لِي فِي ذُرِّيَّتِي ۖ إِنِّي تُبْتُ إِلَيْكَ وَإِنِّي مِنَ الْمُسْلِمِينَ

wa-waṣṣaynā l-'insāna bi-wālidayhi 'iḥsānan ḥamalathu 'ummuhū kurhan wa-waḍa'athu kurhan wa-ḥamluhū wa-fiṣāluhū thalāthūna shahran ḥattā 'idhā balagha 'ashuddahū wa-balagha 'arba'īna sanatan qāla rabbi 'awzi'nī 'an 'ashkura ni'mataka llatī 'an'amta 'alayya wa-'alā wālidayya wa-'an 'a'mala ṣāliḥan tarḍāhu wa-'aṣliḥ lī fī dhurriyyatī 'innī tubtu 'ilayka wa-'innī mina l-muslimīn

15   We have enjoined man to be kind to his parents.
His mother has carried him in travail,
and bore him in travail,
and his gestation and weaning take thirty months.
When he comes of age
and reaches forty years,
     he says, 'My Lord!
Inspire me to give thanks for Your blessing
with which You have blessed me
and my parents,
and that I may do righteous deeds
which may please You,
and invest my descendants with righteousness.
Indeed I have turned to you in penitence,
and I am one of the muslims.'

JUZ 27: adh-Dhariyat 51:31 → Hadid 57:29

49

الْحُجُرَات

50

ق

51

الذَّارِيَات

52

الطُّور

53

النَّجْم

54

الْقَمَر

Qaf

50

Qaf

MECCAN # of Ayas: 45

(1) "Qaf. By the glorious Qur'an"

al-Hujurat

49

Apartments

AKA: The Private Quarters; The Chambers

MEDINAN # of Ayas: 18

(4) "Indeed those who call you from behind the apartments, most of them do not apply reason."

(5) "Had they been patient until you came out for them, it would have been better for them, and Allah is All-Forgiving, All-Merciful."

at-Tur

52

The Mountain

AKA: The Mountain; Mount Tur

MECCAN # of Ayas: 49

(1) "By the Mount [Sinai],"

(2) " by the Book inscribed"

(3) " on an unrolled parchment;"

adh-Dhariyat

51

The Winds That Scatter

AKA: The Dust-Scattering Winds

MECCAN # of Ayas: 60

(1) "By the scattering [winds] that scatter [the clouds];"

(2) "by the [rain] bearing [clouds] laden [with water];"

al-Qamar

54

The Moon

MECCAN # of Ayas: 55

(1) "The Hour has drawn near and the moon is split."

(2) "If they see a sign, they turn away, and say, 'An incessant [powerful] magic!'"

(3) "They denied, and followed their own desires, and every matter has a setting [appropriate to it]."

an-Najm

53

The Star

AKA: The Pleiades

MECCAN # of Ayas: 62

(1) "By the star when it sets:"

(2) "your companion [Muhammad PBUH] has neither gone astray, nor gone amiss."

Make list of Allah's (SWT) creations in nature and marvel at them closely:

Surah 54 (al-Qamar): aya 10

du'a of Nuh (AS)

فَدَعا رَبَّهُ أَنِّي مَغلوبٌ فَانتَصِر

fa-da'ā rabbahū 'annī maghlūbun fa-ntaṣir

10 Thereat he invoked his Lord, [saying,] 'I have been overcome, so help [me].'

JUZ 28: al-Mujadilah 58:1 → at-Tahrim 66:12

Challenge yourself to reach the next level of your recitation!

I want to be able to read/spell ______________________________.

First, I will make du'a!

The next step in reaching this goal is: ______________________________.

And then I will: ____

____, in shaa Allah!

55

الرَّحْمٰن

56

الْوَاقِعَة

57

الْحَدِيد

58

الْمُجَادِلَة

59

الْحَشْر

60

الْمُمْتَحَنَة

al-Waqi'ah 56

The Imminent

AKA: The Inevitable; The Indisputable Event

MECCAN # of Ayas: 96

(1) "When the Imminent [Hour] befalls [That is, the Day of Resurrection and Judgement]"

(2) "-there is no denying that it will befall-"

ar-Rahman 55

The All-Merciful

AKA: The Beneficient; The Most Gracious

MEDINAN # of Ayas: 78

(1) "The All-Beneficent"

(2) "has taught the Qur'an"

(3) "He created man"

(4) "[and] taught him articulate speech."

al-Mujadilah 58

The Pleader

AKA: Woman Who Pleads

MEDINAN # of Ayas: 22

(1) " Allah has certainly heard the speech of her who pleads with you about her husband and complains to Allah. Allah hears the conversation between the two of you. Indeed Allah is All-Hearing, All-Seeing."

al-Hadid 57

Iron

MEDINAN # of Ayas: 29

(25) "Certainly We sent Our apostles with manifest proofs, and We sent down with them the Book and the Balance, so that mankind may maintain justice; and We sent down iron, in which there is great might and uses for mankind, and so that Allah may know those who help Him and His apostles in [their] absence. Indeed Allah is All-Strong, All-Mighty."

al-Mumtahanah 60

The Woman Tested

AKA: She Who Is Tested; The Women Tried

MEDINAN # of Ayas: 13

(10) "O you who have faith! When faithful women come to you as immigrants, test them. Allah knows best [the state of] their faith. Then, if you ascertain them to be faithful women, do not send them back to the faithless. They are not lawful for them, nor are they lawful for them. And give them what they have spent [for them]. There is no sin upon you in marrying them when you have given them their dowries. Do not hold on to [conjugal] ties with faithless women. Ask [the infidels] for what you have spent, and let the faithless ask for what they have spent. That is the judgment of Allah; He judges between you; and Allah is All-Knowing, All-Wise."

al-Hashr 59

The Banishment

AKA: Exile; The Gathering; Confrontation

MEDINAN # of Ayas: 24

(3) " If Allah had not ordained banishment for them, He would have surely punished them in this world, and in the Hereafter there is for them the punishment of the Fire."

Surah 55 (ar-Rahman): aya 60

وَهَل جَزاءُ الإِحسانِ إِلَّا الإِحسانُ

hal jazāʾu l-ʾiḥsāni ʾillā l-ʾiḥsān

60 Is the requital (reward) for goodness anything but goodness?

Surah 60 (al-Mumtahanah): aya 4-5

du'a of Ibraheem (AS)

قَد كانَت لَكُم أُسوَةٌ حَسَنَةٌ في إِبراهيمَ وَالَّذينَ مَعَهُ إِذ قالوا لِقَومِهِم إِنّا
بُرَآءُ مِنكُم وَمِمّا تَعبُدونَ مِن دونِ اللَّهِ كَفَرنا بِكُم وَبَدا بَينَنا وَبَينَكُمُ
العَداوَةُ وَالبَغضاءُ أَبَدًا حَتّىٰ تُؤمِنوا بِاللَّهِ وَحدَهُ إِلّا قَولَ إِبراهيمَ لِأَبيهِ
لَأَستَغفِرَنَّ لَكَ وَما أَملِكُ لَكَ مِنَ اللَّهِ مِن شَيءٍ ۖ رَبَّنا عَلَيكَ تَوَكَّلنا
وَإِلَيكَ أَنَبنا وَإِلَيكَ المَصيرُ

qad kānat lakum ʾuswatun ḥasanatun fī ʾibrāhīma wa-lladhīna maʿahū ʾidh qālū li-qawmihim ʾinnā buraʾāʾu minkum wa-mimmā taʿbudūna min dūni llāhi kafarnā bikum wa-badā baynanā wa-baynakumu l-ʿadāwatu wa-l-baghḍāʾu ʾabadan ḥattā tuʾminū bi-llāhi waḥdahū ʾillā qawla ʾibrāhīma li-ʾabīhi la-ʾastaghfiranna laka wa-mā ʾamliku laka mina llāhi min shayʾin rabbanā ʿalayka tawakkalnā wa-ʾilayka ʾanabnā wa-ʾilayka l-maṣīr

4 There is certainly a good exemplar for you
in Ibraheem
and those who were with him,
when they said to their own people,
'Indeed we repudiate you
and whatever you worship besides Allah.
We disavow you,
and between you and us there has appeared
enmity and hate for ever,
unless you come to have faith in Allah alone,'
except for Abraham's saying to his father,
'I will surely plead forgiveness for you,
though I cannot avail you anything against Allah.'

'Our Lord! In You do we put our trust,
and to You do we turn penitently,
and toward You is the destination.

رَبَّنا لا تَجعَلنا فِتنَةً لِلَّذينَ كَفَروا وَاغفِر لَنا رَبَّنا ۖ إِنَّكَ أَنتَ العَزيزُ الحَكيمُ

rabbanā lā tajʿalnā fitnatan li-lladhīna kafarū wa-ghfir lanā rabbanā ʾinnaka ʾanta l-ʿazīzu l-ḥakīm

JUZ 28: al-Mujadilah 58:1 → at-Tahrim 66:12

Hadith on Rewards of Reciting the Qur'an

Abdullah ibn Mas'ud reported:
The Messenger of Allah, peace and blessings be upon him, said,
"Whoever recites a letter from the Book of Allah, he will receive one good deed as ten good deeds like it. I do not say that Alif Lam Mim is one letter, but rather Alif is a letter, Lam is a letter, and Mim is a letter."

Source: Sunan al-Tirmidhi 29:10 **Grade:** Sahih (authentic) according to Al-Arna'ut

Check off the number of days in a row you read at least 1 letter:

☐ 5 ☐ 10 ☐ 15 ☐ 20 ☐ 25

61

الصَّفّ

62

الْجُمُعَة

63

الْمُنَافِقُون

64

التَّغَابُن

65

الطَّلَاق

66

التَّحْرِيم

al-Jumu'ah 62

Friday

AKA: The Day of Congregation

MEDINAN # of Ayas: 11

(9) "O you who have faith! When the call is made for prayer on Friday, hurry toward the remembrance of Allah, and leave all business. That is better for you, should you know."

(10) "And when the prayer is finished disperse through the land and seek Allah's grace, and remember Allah greatly so that you may be felicitous."

as-Saff 61

Ranks

AKA: The Formations; The Solid Ranks

MEDINAN # of Ayas: 14

(4) "Indeed Allah loves those who fight in His way in ranks, as if they were a compact structure."

at-Taghabun 64

Dispossession

AKA: Mutual Fraud; Profit and Loss

MEDINAN # of Ayas: 18

(9) "The Day when He will gather you for the Day of Gathering, that will be a day of dispossession. And whoever has faith in Allah and acts righteously, He shall absolve him of his misdeeds and admit him into gardens with streams running in them, to remain in them forever. That is the great success."

al-Munafiqun 63

The Hypocrites

MEDINAN # of Ayas: 11

(1) " When the hypocrites come to you they say, 'We bear witness that you are indeed the apostle of Allah.' Allah knows that you are indeed His Apostle, and Allah bears witness that the hypocrites are indeed liars."

at-Tahrim 66

The Forbidding

AKA: The Prohibition

MEDINAN # of Ayas: 12

(1) "O Prophet! Why do you prohibit [yourself] what Allah has made lawful for you, seeking to please your wives? And Allah is All-Forgiving, All-Merciful."

at-Talaq 65

Divorce

MEDINAN # of Ayas: 12

(1) "O Prophet! When you divorce women, divorce them at [the conclusion of] their term and calculate the term, and be wary of Allah, your Lord. Do not turn them out from their houses, nor shall they go out, unless they commit a gross indecency. These are Allah's bounds, and whoever transgresses the bounds of Allah certainly wrongs himself. You never know maybe Allah will bring off something new later on."

Surah 66 (at-Tahrim): aya 8

يا أَيُّهَا الَّذينَ آمَنوا توبوا إِلَى اللَّهِ تَوبَةً نَصوحًا عَسىٰ رَبُّكُم أَن يُكَفِّرَ
عَنكُم سَيِّئَاتِكُم وَيُدخِلَكُم جَنّاتٍ تَجري مِن تَحتِهَا الأَنهارُ يَومَ لا يُخزِي
اللَّهُ النَّبِيَّ وَالَّذينَ آمَنوا مَعَهُ نورُهُم يَسعىٰ بَينَ أَيديهِم وَبِأَيمانِهِم يَقولونَ
رَبَّنا أَتمِم لَنا نورَنا وَاغفِر لَنا إِنَّكَ عَلىٰ كُلِّ شَيءٍ قَديرٌ

yā-ʾayyuhā lladhīna ʾāmanū tūbū ʾilā llāhi tawbatan naṣūḥan ʿasā rabbukum ʾan yukaffira ʿankum sayyiʾātikum wa-yudkhilakum jannātin tajrī min taḥtihā l-ʾanhāru yawma lā yukhzī llāhu n-nabiyya wa-lladhīna ʾāmanū maʿahū nūruhum yasʿā bayna ʾaydīhim wa-bi-ʾaymānihim yaqūlūna rabbanā ʾatmim lanā nūranā wa-ghfir lanā ʾinnaka ʿalā kulli shayʾin qadīr

8 O you who have faith!
Repent to Allah with sincere repentance!
Maybe your Lord
will absolve you of your misdeeds
and admit you into gardens
with streams running in them,
on the day
when Allah will not let the Prophet down
and the faithful who are with him.
Their light will move swiftly before them
and on their right.
They will say, 'Our Lord!
Perfect our light for us, and forgive us!
Indeed You have power over all things.'

Surah 66 (at-Tahrim): aya 11
du'a of Asiya (RA)

وَضَرَبَ اللَّهُ مَثَلًا لِلَّذينَ آمَنُوا امرَأَتَ فِرعَونَ إِذ قالَت رَبِّ ابنِ لي
عِندَكَ بَيتًا فِي الجَنَّةِ وَنَجِّني مِن فِرعَونَ وَعَمَلِهِ وَنَجِّني مِنَ القَومِ الظّالِمينَ

wa-ḍaraba llāhu mathalan li-lladhīna ʾāmanū mraʾata firʿawna ʾidh qālat rabbi bni lī ʿindaka baytan fī l-jannati wa-najjinī min firʿawna wa-ʿamalihī wa-najjinī mina l-qawmi ẓ-ẓālimīn

11 Allah draws an[other] example
for those who have faith:
the wife of Pharaoh, when she said,
'My Lord! Build me a home near You in paradise,
and deliver me from Pharaoh and his conduct,
and deliver me from the wrongdoing lot.'

JUZ 29: al-Mulk 67:1 → al-Mursalat 77:50

BRIEF NOTES:

Surah 71: Nuh (AS)

Prophet Nuh (AS) pleads with his people for more than 900 years to abandon worshipping their gods and to worship Allah (SWT) alone. They refuse so they are punished with a severe flood. Prophet Nuh (AS) is mentioned frequently: 11:25-6; 7:64,72; 11:42-43

67

الْمُلْك

68

الْقَلَم

69

الْحَاقَّة

70

الْمَعَارِج

71

نُوح

72

الْجِنّ

al-Qalam 68

The Pen

MECCAN # of Ayas: 52

(1) "By the Pen and what they write:"
(2) " you are not, by your Lord's blessing, crazy,"
(3) "and yours indeed will be an everlasting reward,"
(4) " and indeed you possess a great character."

al-Mulk 67

Sovereignty

AKA: Control; The Dominion; The Kingdom

MECCAN # of Ayas: 30

(1) "Blessed is He in whose hands is all sovereignty, and He has power over all things."
(2) "He, who created death and life that He may test you [to see] which of you is best in conduct. And He is the All-Mighty, the All-Forgiving."

al-Ma'arij 70

The Ascending Steps

AKA: The Heavenly Ascents; Staircases Upward

MECCAN # of Ayas: 44

(1) "An asker asked for a punishment bound to befall"
(2) "—which none can avert from the faithless—"
(3) "from Allah, Lord of the lofty stations."

al-Haqqah 69

The Inevitable Hour

AKA: The Sure Occurrence; The Undeniable

MECCAN # of Ayas: 52

(13) "When the Trumpet is blown with a single blast"
(14) "and the earth and the mountains are lifted and levelled with a single leveling,"
(15) "then, on that day, will the Imminent [Hour] befall"

al-Jinn 72

The Jinn

AKA: The Spirits; The Unseen Beings

MECCAN # of Ayas: 28

(1) "Say, 'It has been revealed to me that a team of the jinn listened [to the Qur'an].' and they said, "Indeed we heard a wonderful Qur'an'"
(2) "which guides to rectitude. Hence we have believed in it and we will never ascribe any partner to our Lord.'"

Nuh 71

Noah

MECCAN # of Ayas: 28

(1) "Indeed We sent Nuh to his people, [saying,] 'Warn your people before a painful punishment overtakes them.'"

How many of the verified prophets of Allah (SWT) can you name?

There are 25 mentioned in the Qur'an!

Make an effort to get more connected with them.

Prophet ______________ (AS)

Prophet ______________ (AS)

Prophet ______________ (AS)

Prophet ______________ (AS)

Prophet ______________ (AS)

Prophet ______________ (AS)

Prophet ______________ (AS)

Prophet ______________ (AS)

Prophet ______________ (AS)

Prophet ______________ (AS)

Prophet ______________ (AS)

Prophet ______________ (AS)

Prophet ______________ (AS)

Prophet ______________ (AS)

Prophet ______________ (AS)

Prophet ______________ (AS)

Prophet ______________ (AS)

Prophet ______________ (AS)

Prophet ______________ (AS)

Prophet ______________ (AS)

Prophet ______________ (AS)

Prophet ______________ (AS)

Prophet ______________ (AS)

Prophet ______________ (AS)

Prophet ______________ (AS)

Surah 71 (Nuh) (AS): aya 28

du'a of Nuh (AS)

رَبِّ اغفِر لي وَلِوالِدَيَّ وَلِمَن دَخَلَ بَيتِيَ مُؤمِنًا وَلِلمُؤمِنينَ

وَالمُؤمِناتِ وَلا تَزِدِ الظّالِمينَ إِلّا تَبارًا

rabbi ghfir lī wa-li-wālidayya wa-li-man dakhala baytiya muʾminan wa-li-l-muʾminīna wa-l-muʾmināti wa-lā tazidi ẓ-ẓālimīna ʾillā tabāra

28 My Lord! Forgive me and my parents,
and whoever enters my house in faith,
and the faithful men and women,
and do not increase the wrongdoers in anything
except ruin.'

MABROOK! CONGRATULATIONS!

You've made it nearly **one third** of the way!

Alhamdullilah! (All praise is due to Allah!)

KEEP GOING! You can do it! in shaa Allah (God-Willing)

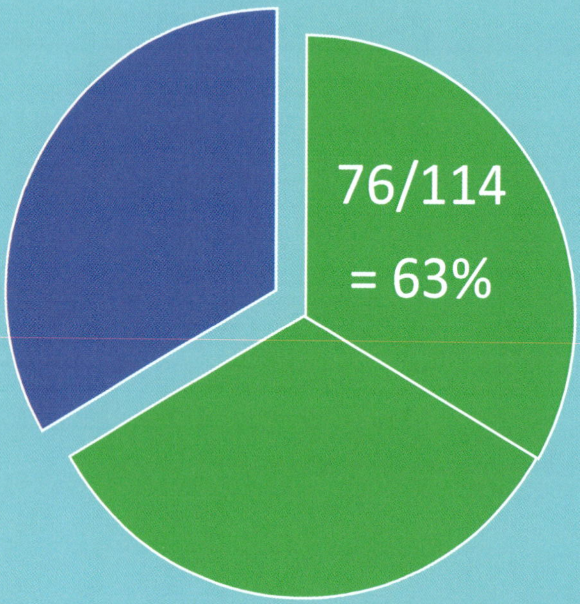

MY PROGRESS CHART for the LAST 37%! 😊😊😊

73		74		75		76		77		78	
Number:		Number:		Number:		Number:		Number:		Number:	
English:		English:		English:		English:		English:		English:	
Arabic:		Arabic:		Arabic:		Arabic:		Arabic:		Arabic:	
Aya:		Aya:		Aya:		Aya:		Aya:		Aya:	

79		80		81		82		83		84	
Number:		Number:		Number:		Number:		Number:		Number:	
English:		English:		English:		English:		English:		English:	
Arabic:		Arabic:		Arabic:		Arabic:		Arabic:		Arabic:	
Aya:		Aya:		Aya:		Aya:		Aya:		Aya:	

85		86		87		88		89		90	
Number:		Number:		Number:		Number:		Number:		Number:	
English:		English:		English:		English:		English:		English:	
Arabic:		Arabic:		Arabic:		Arabic:		Arabic:		Arabic:	
Aya:		Aya:		Aya:		Aya:		Aya:		Aya:	

91		92		93		94		95		96	
Number:		Number:		Number:		Number:		Number:		Number:	
English:		English:		English:		English:		English:		English:	
Arabic:		Arabic:		Arabic:		Arabic:		Arabic:		Arabic:	
Aya:		Aya:		Aya:		Aya:		Aya:		Aya:	

97		98		99		100		101		102	
Number:		Number:		Number:		Number:		Number:		Number:	
English:		English:		English:		English:		English:		English:	
Arabic:		Arabic:		Arabic:		Arabic:		Arabic:		Arabic:	
Aya:		Aya:		Aya:		Aya:		Aya:		Aya:	

103		104		105		106		107		108	
Number:		Number:		Number:		Number:		Number:		Number:	
English:		English:		English:		English:		English:		English:	
Arabic:		Arabic:		Arabic:		Arabic:		Arabic:		Arabic:	
Aya:		Aya:		Aya:		Aya:		Aya:		Aya:	

JUZ 29: al-Mulk 67:1 → al-Mursalat 77:50

What stands out to you as the best possible habits of a believer?

How can you increase your efforts of charity in your everyday life?

I can smile more (be friendlier) when I

I can donate my time by volunteering, making something and giving it away, cooking extra food and sharing, helping someone with their [home]work and...

I can take care of my body and my health by

I can help others by

73

الْمُزَّمِّل

74

الْمُدَّثِّر

75

الْقِيَامَة

76

الْإِنْسَان

77

الْمُرْسَلَات

78

النَّبَأ

al-Muddath-thir 74

Shrouded

AKA: The Man Wearing A Cloak

MECCAN # of Ayas: 56

(1) " O you wrapped up in your mantle!"
(2) "Rise up and warn!"
(3) "Magnify your Lord,"
(4) "and purify your cloak,
(5) "and keep away from all impurity!"

al-Muzzammil 73

Enwrapped

AKA: Folded in Garments; Bundled Up

MECCAN # of Ayas: 20

(1) "O you wrapped up in your mantle!"
(2) "Stand vigil through the night, except a little,"
(3) "a half, or reduce a little from that"

al-Insan 76

The Human

AKA: Every (Man)

MEDINAN # of Ayas: 31

(1) "Has there been for man a period of time when he was not anything worthy of mention?"
(2) "Indeed We created man from the drop of a mixed fluid so that We may test him. So We made him endowed with hearing and sight."

al-Qiyamah 75

Resurrection

AKA: Day of Resurrection; The Rising

MECCAN # of Ayas: 40

(1) "I swear by the Day of Resurrection!"
(2) "And I swear by the self-blaming soul!"
(3) "Does man suppose that We shall not put together his bones?"

an-Naba 78

The Great Tiding

AKA: The Announcement; The Important News

MECCAN # of Ayas: 40

(1) "What is it about which they question each other?!"
(2) "[Is it] about the great tiding,"
(3) "the one about which they differ?"

al-Mursalat 77

Those Sent Forth

AKA: The Emissaries

MECCAN # of Ayas: 50

(1) "By the successive emissaries,"
(2) "by the raging hurricanes,"

Surah 73 (al-Muzzamil): ayat 19-20

إِنَّ هٰذِهِ تَذكِرَةٌ ۖ فَمَن شاءَ اتَّخَذَ إِلىٰ رَبِّهِ سَبيلًا

ʾinna hādhihī tadhkiratun fa-man shāʾa ttakhadha ʾilā rabbihī sabīla

19 This is indeed a reminder.
So let anyone who wishes take the way toward his Lord.

إِنَّ رَبَّكَ يَعلَمُ أَنَّكَ تَقومُ أَدنىٰ مِن ثُلُثَيِ اللَّيلِ وَنِصفَهُ وَثُلُثَهُ وَطائِفَةٌ مِنَ
الَّذينَ مَعَكَ ۚ وَاللَّهُ يُقَدِّرُ اللَّيلَ وَالنَّهارَ ۚ عَلِمَ أَن لَن تُحصوهُ فَتابَ
عَلَيكُم ۖ فَاقرَءوا ما تَيَسَّرَ مِنَ القُرآنِ ۚ عَلِمَ أَن سَيَكونُ مِنكُم مَرضىٰ ۙ
وَآخَرونَ يَضرِبونَ فِي الأَرضِ يَبتَغونَ مِن فَضلِ اللَّهِ ۙ وَآخَرونَ يُقاتِلونَ في
سَبيلِ اللَّهِ ۖ فَاقرَءوا ما تَيَسَّرَ مِنهُ ۚ وَأَقيمُوا الصَّلاةَ وَآتُوا الزَّكاةَ وَأَقرِضُوا
اللَّهَ قَرضًا حَسَنًا ۚ وَما تُقَدِّموا لِأَنفُسِكُم مِن خَيرٍ تَجِدوهُ عِندَ اللَّهِ هُوَ
خَيرًا وَأَعظَمَ أَجرًا ۚ وَاستَغفِرُوا اللَّهَ ۖ إِنَّ اللَّهَ غَفورٌ رَحيمٌ

ʾinna rabbaka yaʿlamu ʾannaka taqūmu ʾadnā min thuluthayi l-layli wa-niṣfahū wa-thuluthahū wa-ṭāʾifatun mina lladhīna maʿaka wa-llāhu yuqaddiru l-layla wa-n-nahāra ʿalima ʾan lan tuḥṣūhu fa-tāba ʿalaykum fa-qraʾū mā tayassara mina l-qurʾāni ʿalima ʾan sa-yakūnu minkum marḍā wa-ʾākharūna yaḍribūna fī l-ʾarḍi yabtaghūna min faḍli llāhi wa-ʾākharūna yuqātilūna fī sabīli llāhi fa-qraʾū mā tayassara minhu wa-ʾaqīmū ṣ-ṣalāta wa-ʾātū z-zakāta wa-ʾaqriḍū llāha qarḍan ḥasanan wa-mā tuqaddimū li-ʾanfusikum min khayrin tajidūhu ʿinda llāhi huwa khayran wa-ʾaʿẓama ʾajran wa-staghfirū llāha ʾinna llāha ghafūrun raḥīm

20 Indeed your Lord knows
that you stand vigil nearly two thirds of the night
—or [at times] a half or a third of it—
along with a group of those who are with you.
Allah measures the night and the day.
He knows that you cannot calculate it [exactly],
and so He was lenient toward you.
So recite as much of the Qur'ān as is feasible.
He knows that some of you will be sick,
while others will travel in the land
seeking Allah's grace,
and yet others will fight in the way of Allah.
So recite as much of it as is feasible,
and maintain the prayer and pay the zakāt
and lend Allah a good loan.
Whatever good you send ahead for your souls
you will find it with Allah [in a form]
that is better and greater with respect to reward.
And plead to Allah for forgiveness;
indeed Allah is All-Forgiving, All-Merciful.

JUZ 30: an-Naba 78:1 → an-Nas 114:6

You made it to the final juz of the Qur'an!

Find a way to share what you're learning with others.

Take time to find an in-person or online group of learners to join:

79

النَّازِعَات

80

عَبَسَ

81

التَّكْوِير

82

الْإِنْفِطَار

83

الْمُطَفِّفِين

84

الْإِنْشِقَاق

'Abasa 80

He Frowned

AKA: He Made A Wry Face; He Who Frowned

MECCAN # of Ayas: 42

(1) "He frowned and turned away"

(2) "when the blind man approached him."

(3) "And how do you know, maybe he would purify himself,"

(4) "or take admonition, and the admonition would benefit him!"

an-Naazi'at 79

Extractors

AKA: The Wresters; The Angelic Pullers

MECCAN # of Ayas: 46

(1) "By those [angels] who wrest [the soul] violently,"

(2) "by those who draw [it] out gently,"

al-Infitar 82

The Rending

AKA: The Splitting; Torn Apart

MECCAN # of Ayas: 19

(1) "When the sky is rent [torn] apart,"

at-Takwir 81

The Darkening

AKA: The Winding Up; The Folding Up

MECCAN # of Ayas: 29

(1) "When the sun is wound up [Or 'turns dark.']"

al-Inshiqaq 84

The Splitting

AKA: Bursting Asunder; Ripped Apart

MECCAN # of Ayas: 25

(1) "When the sky is split open"

(2) "and gives ear to its Lord as it should."

(3) "When the earth is spread out"

(4) "and throws out what is in it, emptying itself,

(5) "and gives ear to its Lord as it should."

al-Mutaffifeen 83

The Defrauders

AKA: Those who Give Short Measure

MECCAN # of Ayas: 36

(1) "Woe to the defrauders who use short measures,"

(2) "who, when they measure [a commodity bought] from the people, take the full measure,"

(3) "but diminish when they measure or weigh for them."

Surah 82 (al-Infitar): ayat 17-19

وَما أَدراكَ ما يَومُ الدّينِ

wa-mā 'adrāka mā yawmu d-dīn

17 And what will show you
what is the Day of Retribution?

ثُمَّ ما أَدراكَ ما يَومُ الدّينِ

thumma mā 'adrāka mā yawmu d-dīn

18 Again, what will show
you what is the Day of Retribution?

يَومَ لا تَملِكُ نَفسٌ لِنَفسٍ شَيئًا ۖ وَالأَمرُ يَومَئِذٍ لِلَّهِ

yawma lā tamliku nafsun li-nafsin shay'an wa-l-'amru yawma'idhin li-llāh

19 It is a day
when no soul will be of any avail to another soul
and all command that day will belong to Allah.

Allah (SWT) warns mankind of the coming of the Day (Day of Judgement; Day of Resurrection; Day of Retribution) many, many times.

What details have you learned so far?

1. ______________________________

2. ______________________________

3. ______________________________

4. ______________________________

5. ______________________________

6. ______________________________

7. ______________________________

8. ______________________________

9. ______________________________

10. ______________________________

May Allah have mercy on us all!

85

الْبُرُوج

86

الطَّارِق

87

الْأَعْلَىٰ

88

الْغَاشِيَة

89

الْفَجْر

90

الْبَلَد

at-Tariq 86

The Nightly Visitor

AKA: The Nightcomer

MECCAN # of Ayas: 17

(1) "By the sky, by the nightly visitor,"
(2) "(and what will show you what is the nightly visitor?"
(3) "It is the brilliant star):"
(4) "there is a guard over every soul."

al-Buruj 85

The Houses

AKA: The Constellations

MECCAN # of Ayas: 22

(1) "By the sky with its houses [constellations],"

al-Ghashiyah 88

The Overwhelmer

AKA: The Overpowering; The Whelming

MECCAN # of Ayas: 26

(2) "Some faces on that day will be humbled,"
(3) "wrought-up and weary:"

al-A'la 87

The Most Exalted

AKA: The Highest; The Most High

MECCAN # of Ayas: 19

(1) "Celebrate the Name of your Lord, the Most Exalted,"

al-Balad 90

The City

AKA: The Earth; The Land; The Town

MECCAN # of Ayas: 20

(1) "I swear by this town,"

...

(5) "Does he suppose that no one will ever have power over him?"
(6) "He says, 'I have squandered immense wealth.'"
(7) "Does he suppose that no one sees him?"

al-Fajr 89

The Dawn

AKA: The Daybreak

MECCAN # of Ayas: 30

(1) "By the Dawn,"
(2) "by the ten nights,"
(3) "by the Even and the Odd,"
(4) "by the night when it departs!"

Surah 87 (al-A'la): ayat 14-15

قَد أَفلَحَ مَن تَزَكّىٰ

qad 'aflaḥa man tazakkā

14 Felicitous is he who purifies himself,

وَذَكَرَ اسمَ رَبِّهِ فَصَلّىٰ

wa-dhakara sma rabbihī fa-ṣallā

15 celebrates the Name of his Lord, and prays.

Retell the story of the first ayas reveal to Prophet Muhammad (PBUH):

Prophet Muhammad (PBUH) was ___ years old. The angel ________ visited Muhammad (PBUH) at the cave of Hira. He told him to "______." After that, the Prophet Muhammad went home to his wife, __________________ (RA), and told her" _______________________" which means "____________________________."

The verses first revealed are:

____

____

____

____

91

الشَّمْس

92

اللَّيل

93

الضُّحَى

94

الشَّرْح

95

التِّين

96

الْعَلَق

al-Layl

92

The Night

MECCAN # of Ayas: 21

(1) "By the night when it envelops,"

ash-Shams

91

The Sun

MECCAN # of Ayas: 15

(1) "By the sun and her forenoon splendour,"

ash-Sharh

94

The Opening of the Heart

AKA: Comfort; Relief; The Expansion

MECCAN # of Ayas: 8

(1) "Did We not open your breast for you"

(2) "and relieve you of your burden"

(3) "which [almost] broke your back?"

ad-Duha

93

The Morning Brightness

AKA: Early Hours of the Morning; The Glorious Morning Light

MECCAN # of Ayas: 11

(1) "By the morning brightness,"

(2) "by the night when it is calm!"

al-'Alaq

96

The Clinging Mass

AKA: The Embryo; The Clinging Clot; Read

MECCAN # of Ayas: 19

(1) "Read in the Name of your Lord who created;"

(2) "created man from a clinging mass."

at-Tin

95

The Fig

AKA: The Figtree

MECCAN # of Ayas: 8

(1) "By the fig and the olive,"

BRIEF NOTES:

Surah 96: al-'Alaq (the Clinging Mass)

The first ayas from the entire Qur'an were revealed to Prophet Muhammad (peace and blessings be upon him) at the cave of Hira

Surah 96 (al-'Alaq): ayat 1-5

اقرَأ بِاسمِ رَبِّكَ الَّذي خَلَقَ

iqra' bi-smi rabbika lladhī khalaq

1 Read in the Name of your Lord who created;

خَلَقَ الإِنسانَ مِن عَلَقٍ

khalaqa l-'insāna min 'alaqi

2 created man from a clinging mass.

اقرَأ وَرَبُّكَ الأَكرَمُ

iqra' wa-rabbuka l-'akram

3 Read and your Lord is the most generous,

الَّذي عَلَّمَ بِالقَلَمِ

alladhī 'allama bi-l-qalam

4 who taught by the pen,

لَّمَ الإِنسانَ ما لَم يَعلَم

'allama l-'insāna mā lam ya'lam

5 taught man what he did not know.

Surah 94 (ash-Sharh): ayat 5-8

فَإِنَّ مَعَ العُسرِ يُسرًا

fa-'inna ma'a l-'usri Yusra

5 Indeed ease accompanies hardship.

ثإِنَّ مَعَ العُسرِ يُسرًا

'inna ma'a l-'usri yusra

6 Indeed ease accompanies hardship.

فَإِذا فَرَغتَ فَانصَب

fa-'idhā faraghta fa-nṣa

7 When you are finished [with prayer], exert yourself [in supplicating to Allah].

وَإِلىٰ رَبِّكَ فَارغَب

wa-'ilā rabbika fa-rghab

8 and turn eagerly to your Lord.

Jot down some of your plans to increase your worship and make good use of your time next Ramadan, in shaa Allah (God-willing)!

Prayer (late-night, early morning, Sunnah?):

Dhikr (remembrance of Allah (SWT)):

Qur'an (amount everyday; total amount during the month):

97

الْقَدر

98

الْبَيِّنَة

99

الزَّلْزَلَة

100

الْعَاديَات

101

الْقَارِعَة

102

التَكَاثُر

al-Bayyinah 98

The Clear Proof

AKA: The Clear Evidence; The Clear Sign

MEDINAN # of Ayas: 8

(1) "The faithless from among the People of the Book and the polytheists were not set apart until the proof had come to them:"

(2) "an apostle from Allah reciting impeccable scriptures,"

(3) "wherein are upright writings." ...

al-Qadr 97

The Night of Power

AKA: The Night of Glory; Determination

MECCAN # of Ayas: 5

(1) "Indeed We sent it [the Qur'an] down on the Night of Ordainment."

al-'Adiyat 100

The War Steeds

AKA: The Chargers; The Charging Mares

MECCAN # of Ayas: 11

(1) "By the snorting chargers,"

(2) "by the strikers of sparks [with their hoofs],"

al-Zalzalah 99

The Earthquake

AKA: The Shock; The Quaking

MEDINAN # of Ayas: 8

(1) "When the earth is rocked with a terrible quake"

at-Takathur 102

Worldly Gains

AKA: Striving for More; Worldly Abundance

MECCAN # of Ayas: 8

(1) "Rivalry [and vainglory] distracted you"

(2) "until you visited [even] the graves."

al-Qari'ah 101

The Catastrophe

AKA: The Day of Noise and Clamour

MECCAN # of Ayas: 11

(1) "The Catastrophe!"

(2) "What is the Catastrophe?"

(3) "What will show you what is the Catastrophe?"

(4) "The day mankind will be like scattered moths,"

(5) "and the mountains will be like carded wool."

Surah 97 (al-Qadr): ayat 1-5

إِنَّا أَنزَلناهُ فِي لَيلَةِ القَدرِ

'innā 'anzalnāhu fī laylati l-qadr

1 Indeed We sent it [the Qur'an] down on the Night of Ordainment.

وَما أَدراكَ ما لَيلَةُ القَدرِ

wa-mā 'adrāka mā laylatu l-qadr

2 What will show you what is the Night of Ordainment?

لَيلَةُ القَدرِ خَيرٌ مِن أَلفِ شَهرٍ

laylatu l-qadri khayrun min 'alfi shahr

3 The Night of Ordainment is better than a thousand months.

تَنَزَّلُ المَلائِكَةُ وَالرّوحُ فيها بِإِذنِ رَبِّهِم مِن كُلِّ أَمرٍ

tanazzalu l-malā'ikatu wa-r-rūḥu fīhā bi-'idhni rabbihim min kulli 'amr

4 In it the angels and the spirit descend, by the leave of their Lord, with every command.

سَلامٌ هِيَ حَتّىٰ مَطلَعِ الفَجرِ

salāmun hiya ḥattā maṭla'i l-fajr

5 It is peaceful until the rising of the dawn.

TIME FOR SOME GRATITUDE!

There is literally an innumerable amount of things to be grateful for in this life!
Can you find 20 in your life?

1. ______________________________
2. ______________________________
3. ______________________________
4. ______________________________
5. ______________________________
6. ______________________________
7. ______________________________
8. ______________________________
9. ______________________________
10. ______________________________
11. ______________________________
12. ______________________________
13. ______________________________
14. ______________________________
15. ______________________________
16. ______________________________
17. ______________________________
18. ______________________________
19. ______________________________
20. ______________________________

103

الْعَصْر

104

الْهُمَزَة

105

الفِيل

106

قُرَيْش

107

الْمَاعُون

108

الْكَوْثَر

al-Humazah 104

The Backbiter

AKA: The [Gossipmonger; The Slanderer

MECCAN # of Ayas: 9

(1) "Woe to every scandal-monger and slanderer,"

(2) " who amasses wealth and counts it over."

al-'Asr 103

The Decline of Time

AKA: Time and Age; The Declining Day

MECCAN # of Ayas: 3

(1) "By Time!"

(2) "Indeed man is in loss,"

(3) "except those who have faith and do righteous deeds,
and enjoin one another to [follow] the truth,
and enjoin one another to patience."

Quraysh 106

The Tribe of Quraysh

AKA: The Quraish (Custodians of the Ka'bah)

MECCAN # of Ayas: 4

(1) "For the [accustomed security] among the Quraysh,"

(2) "their solidarity during winter and summer journeys,"

(3) "let them worship the Lord of this House,"

(4) "who has fed them [and saved them] from hunger, and secured them from fear."

al-Fil 105

The Elephant

MECCAN # of Ayas: 5

(1) "Have you not regarded how your Lord dealt with the Men of the Elephant? "

(2) "Did He not make their stratagems go awry,"

(3) "and send against them flocks of birds"

(4) "pelting them with stones of shale,"

(5) "thus making them like chewed-up straw?"

al-Kawthar 108

Abundant Goodness

AKA: Plenty; The Great Abundance

MECCAN # of Ayas: 3

(1) "Indeed We have given you abundance."

(2) "So pray to your Lord, and sacrifice [the sacrificial camel (or raise your hands)]"

(3) "Indeed it is your enemy who is without posterity."

al-Ma'un 107

Helping Others

AKA: Common Kindnesses; Neighborly Needs

MECCAN # of Ayas: 7

(1) "Did you see him who denies the Retribution?"

(2) "That is the one who drives away the orphan,"

(3) "and does not urge the feeding of the needy."

(4) "Woe to them who pray,"

(5) "—those who are heedless of their prayers,"

(6) "those who show off"

(7) "but deny aid"

Surah 103 (al-Asr): ayat 1-3

وَالعَصرِ

wa-l-ʿaṣr

1 By time!

إِنَّ الإِنسانَ لَفي خُسرٍ

ʾinna l-ʾinsāna la-fī khusr

2 Indeed man is in loss,

إِلَّا الَّذينَ آمَنوا وَعَمِلُوا الصّالِحاتِ

وَتَواصَوا بِالحَقِّ وَتَواصَوا بِالصَّبرِ

ʾillā lladhīna ʾāmanū wa-ʿamilū ṣ-ṣāliḥāti
wa-tawāṣaw bi-l-ḥaqqi wa-tawāṣaw bi-ṣ-ṣabr

3 except those who have faith
and do righteous deeds,
and enjoin one another to [follow] the truth,
and enjoin one another to patience

109		110		111		112		113		114	
Number:		Number:		Number:		Number:		Number:		Number:	
English:		English:		English:		English:		English:		English:	
Arabic:		Arabic:		Arabic:		Arabic:		Arabic:		Arabic:	
Aya:		Aya:		Aya:		Aya:		Aya:		Aya:	

THE FINAL 5.2%!

109

الْكَافِرُون

110

النَّصر

111

الْمَسَد

112

الْإخْلَاص

113

الْفَلَق

114

النَّاس

an-Nasr 110

The Help

AKA: (Divine) Support

MEDINAN # of Ayas: 3

(1) *"When Allah's help comes with victory,"*

(2) *"and you see the people entering Allah's religion in throngs,"*

(3) *"then celebrate the praise of your Lord, and plead to Him for forgiveness. Indeed He is All-Clement."*

al-Kafirun 109

The Faithless

AKA: Those Who Reject Faith

MECCAN # of Ayas: 6

(1) *"Say, 'O faithless ones!"*

(2) *"I do not worship what you worship,"*

(3) *"nor do you worship what I worship;"*

(4) *"nor will I worship what you have worshiped"*

(5) *"nor will you worship what I worship."*

(6) *"To you your religion, and to me my religion.'"*

al-Ikhlas 112

Monotheism

AKA: Pure Faith; Divine Unity

MECCAN # of Ayas: 4

(1) *"Say, 'He is Allah, the One."*

(2) *"Allah is the All-Embracing."*

(3) *"He neither begat, nor was begotten,"*

(4) *"nor has He any equal.'"*

al-Masad 111

Palm Fiber

AKA: Abu Lahab; The Palm-Fiber Rope

MECCAN # of Ayas: 5

(1) *"Perish the hands of Abu Lahab and perish he!"*

(2) *"Neither his wealth availed him, nor what he had earned."*

(3) *"Soon he will enter the blazing fire,"*

(4) *"and his wife [too], the firewood carrier [the informer],"*

an-Nas 114

Humankind

AKA: All People; Humans

MECCAN # of Ayas: 6

(1) *"Say, 'I seek the protection of the Lord of humans,"*

(2) *"Sovereign of humans,"*

(3) *"God of humans,"*

(4) *"from the evil of the sneaky tempter"*

(5) *"who puts temptations into the breasts of humans,"*

(6) *"from among the jinn and humans.'"*

al-Falaq 113

The Daybreak

AKA: The Dawn; The Rising Day

MECCAN # of Ayas: 5

(1) *"Say, 'I seek the protection of the Lord of the Daybreak*

(2) *"from the evil of what He has created,"*

(3) *"and from the evil of the dark night when it settles,"*

(4) *"and from the evil of the witches who blow on knots,"*

(5) *"and from the evil of the envious one when he envies.'"*

The 3 Quls for Protection:

Abdullah ibn Khubayb reported:
The Messenger of Allah, peace and blessings be upon him, said, "Speak."
I said, "What should I say?"
The Prophet (PBUH) said, "Say: He is Allah, the One, (112:1)
and the two chapters of refuge, al-Falaq and al-Nas,
every evening and morning three times.
They will be enough for you against everything."

Source: Sunan al-Tirmidhī 3575

Grade: Sahih (authentic) according to Al-Nawawi

Surah 112: al-Ikhlas (Monotheism)

بِسۡمِ اللهِ الرَّحۡمٰنِ الرَّحِيۡمِ
bismillāhi r-raḥmāni r-raḥīm
In the name of Allah, the Beneficent, the Merciful.

قُل هُوَ اللَّهُ أَحَدٌ
qul huwa llāhu 'aḥadun-i
1 Say: He is Allah, the One!

اللَّهُ الصَّمَدُ
Allāhu ṣ-ṣamadu
2 Allah, the eternally Besought of all!

لَم يَلِد وَلَم يولَد
lam yalid wa-lam yūlad
3 He begetteth not nor was begotten.

وَلَم يَكُن لَهُ كُفُوًا أَحَدٌ
wa-lam yakun lahū kufuwan 'aḥadun
4 And there is none comparable unto Him.

Surah 113: al-Falaq (The Daybreak)

بِسۡمِ اللهِ الرَّحۡمٰنِ الرَّحِيۡمِ
bismillāhi r-raḥmāni r-raḥīm
In the name of Allah, the Beneficent, the Merciful.

قُل أَعوذُ بِرَبِّ الفَلَقِ
qul 'a'ūdhu bi-rabbi l-falaqi
1 Say: I seek refuge in the Lord of the Daybreak

مِن شَرِّ ما خَلَقَ
min sharri mā khalaqa
2 From the evil of that which He created;

وَمِن شَرِّ غاسِقٍ إِذا وَقَبَ
wa-min sharri ghāsiqin 'idhā waqaba
3 From the evil of the darkness when it is intense,

وَمِن شَرِّ النَّفّاثاتِ فِي العُقَدِ
wa-min sharri n-naffāthāti fī l-'uqadi
4 And from the evil of malignant witchcraft,

وَمِن شَرِّ حاسِدٍ إِذا حَسَدَ
wa-min sharri ḥāsidin 'idhā ḥasada
5 And from the evil of the envier when he envieth.

Surah 114: an-Nas (Mankind)

بِسۡمِ اللهِ الرَّحۡمٰنِ الرَّحِيۡمِ
bismillāhi r-raḥmāni r-raḥīm
In the name of Allah, the Beneficent, the Merciful.

قُل أَعوذُ بِرَبِّ النّاسِ
qul 'a'ūdhu bi-rabbi n-nās
1 Say, I seek refuge in the Lord of mankind,

مَلِكِ النّاسِ
maliki n-nās
2 The King of mankind,

إِلٰهِ النّاسِ
ilāhi n-nās
3 The God of mankind,

مِن شَرِّ الوَسواسِ الخَنّاسِ
min sharri l-waswāsi l-khannās
4 From the evil of the sneaking whisperer

الَّذي يُوَسوِسُ في صُدورِ النّاسِ
alladhī yuwaswisu fī ṣudūri n-nās
5 Who whispers in the hearts of mankind,

مِنَ الجِنَّةِ وَالنّاسِ
mina l-jinnati wa-n-nāsi
6 Of the jinn and mankind.

SUBHANA ALLAH! GLORY BE TO ALLAH!

You've made it! Alhamdullilah! All praise is due to Allah!

WHAT WILL YOU DO NEXT?

Do it for the sake of Allah (fi sabilillah)!